LONG LIVE SAMSON

WRITTEN AND ILLUSTRATED BY
ALAN HINES

Dedicated to anyone
who has ever loved
and lost an animal friend.

Toddlers to Dodderers Publishing

www.toddlerstododdererspublishing.com

Quality Picture Books for Children and Seniors

LONG LIVE SAMSON

Will Jordan was out rock hunting, in a meadow. He carried a canvas bag to collect the stones he found. The calm afternoon was disrupted by a dog barking.

A few yards away he saw a dog chasing squirrels, in and around a badly rotted, abandoned shed. An old tire lay on the rusted roof.

Will let out a shrill whistle, to get the dog's attention.

Startled by the sharp sound, the dog jerked around and slammed its head into a support post. The wooden pole broke in half.

The entire building collapsed.

KABOOM!

A huge dust cloud filled the air. The dog and the squirrels were running for their lives. The rubber tire, once on the roof top, was chasing all of them!

Will ran over to check on the dog. It was fine and they bonded instantly! Together, the two headed home. Will hoped his parents would allow his new buddy to live there.

After a bath, the dog gobbled up a plate of rice
and gravy and fried chicken, with the bones
removed. He wasn't fond of the green peas however,
and just moved them around with his nose.

Will asked his parents if he might keep the dog.
They informed him, that owning a pet was a huge
responsibility requiring lots of love, attention
and money. Mr. Jordan said, "We will talk
more about this on Saturday.
Tonight your friend may sleep in the garage."

The next morning, Father and son looked in
the newspaper, but found nothing that fit the
dog's description. Mr. Jordan told Will to post an
ad online, and distribute flyers around town describing
him. Then he added, "if no one claims the dog in
two weeks, he's yours."

Two weeks passed. Will celebrated by taking his
pet to the veterinarian for a check up.

Will named him Samson because he had long flowing
hair and knocked a whole building down by himself! He
placed a collar on his pal, with a tag bearing the name.

During the school year, Samson greeted Will with a kiss at the bus stop every afternoon.

After the homework was finished, they watched television together until bedtime.

In the Spring,

the two went swimming in a nearby creek.

In the Summer,

they played Frisbee in the park.

In the Fall,

Samson helped with the leaf raking.

In the Winter,

they built snowmen. Going home for
hot chocolate afterwards was the best part!

In late October, Will and Samson carved
Jack-O-Lanterns for Halloween.

During the Christmas season,
Samson assisted Will with the tree lights.

The years passed. They had grown very close. Samson was
a member of the family and slept on a rug next to Will's bed.

One morning, while Will was in school,
a neighbor came to the door and
gave Mrs. Jordan some terrible news.
While driving, Samson had darted out in front of
his car. He wasn't able to stop in time,
so he struck Samson. Mrs. Jordan wept,
because she also loved Samson, and
wondered how she would tell Will that
his best friend was gone.

That afternoon, when Samson was not at the bus stop, Will ran home to find him. His Mom told him the sad news, and he was heart broken.

He grieved over the loss of his friend for a
long time, and went to places they had played
together. He had an empty feeling inside.

Feeling very lonely, Will lay awake nights thinking about, and missing Samson. Often a distant train horn sounded sad as well.

One cold, dark night Will awakened to a dream-like light, streaming through the windows. Dashing over to look, his heart pounded with excitement. Samson, was surrounded with brilliant, glowing rays, happily chasing squirrels.

Ever since that night, Will never worried about Samson again, because of the wonderful dream he had.
Or ...

Was it a dream?

Acknowledgements

My sincere appreciation to the following individuals whose knowledge and efforts contributed to the creation of this book.

Charles Hoffman...Editor

Suzanne LaValley-Hines............................Layout Artist

Jay Javan... Mock-up Artist

Stephen Fitzgerald............................ PDF File Creator

Figure Models
(In Order of Appearance)

Jon Patrick...Will Whistling

Bill Jarrett...Mr. Jordan

Charles Hoffman............................Distraught Neighbor

Ann Marie Jarrett.......................................Mrs. Jordan

Special Thanks to My Mother

Frances Hines is the reason a little story I created years ago, evolved into the book you are holding.

Save a life and make a friend. Adopt a pet from your local shelter. Keep them healthy with regular veterinary visits, and remember to be kind to all animals.

www.toddlerstododdererspublishing.com